Japan

Japan has been called the world's most rapidly changing society. But at the same time, as many of the interviews in this book show, Japan still rests upon traditions reaching back into the mists of time. It is this balance of tradition with rapid change that makes Japan unique among other nations of the world.

For Japan has undergone two major transformations in the last hundred years: first in the nineteenth century when the country abolished the stagnant feudal system and embarked on the road to modernization; and again in the mid-twentieth century when it turned away from the tragic experience of World War II to create a new, highly industrialized society dedicated to peaceful cooperation and democracy. Both of these changes were accomplished without discarding the traditional culture and customs of the country.

In *We Live in Japan*, a cross-section of the Japanese people tell you what their life is like – life in the city, on the coast, in the mountains, in the countryside.

The author, Kazuhide Kawamata, is a freelance writer and photographer. He has traveled extensively throughout Japan and now lives in Tokyo.

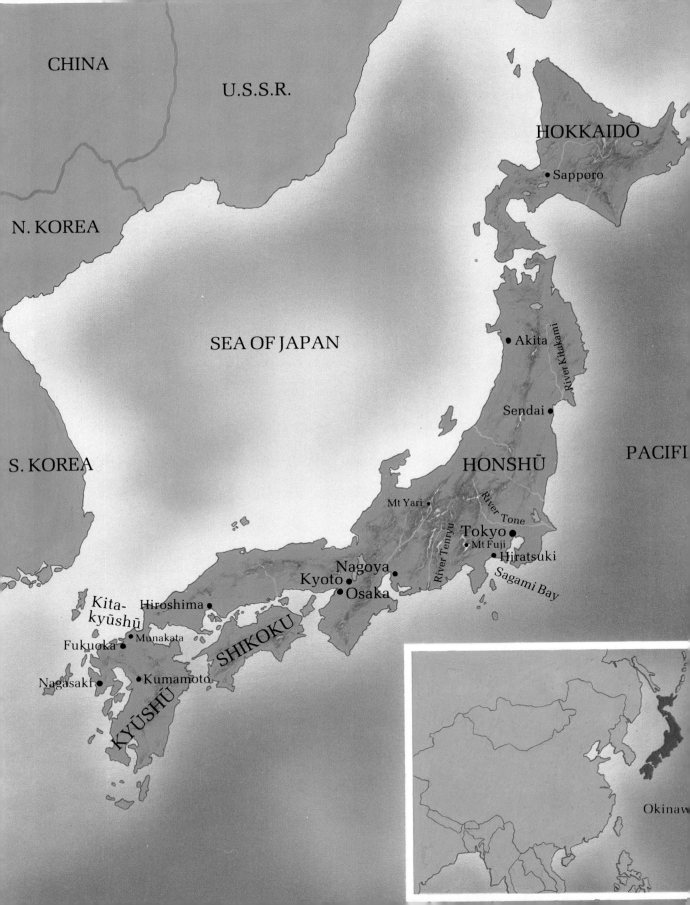

we live in
JAPAN

Kazuhide Kawamata

The Bookwright Press
New York · 1984

Living Here

We live in Argentina
We live in Australia
We live in Britain
We live in China
We live in Denmark
We live in France
We live in Greece
We live in India

We live in Israel
We live in Italy
We live in Japan
We live in Kenya
We live in New Zealand
We live in Spain
We live in West Germany

First published in the United States in 1984 by
The Bookwright Press
387 Park Avenue South
New York, N.Y. 10016

First published in Great Brtain in 1984 by
Wayland (Publishers) Ltd
49 Lansdowne Place, Hove
East Sussex BN3 1HF, England

ISBN 0–531–03796–7
Library of Congress Catalog Card Number: 84–70774

Printed by G. Canale & C.S.p.A., Turin, Italy

Contents

"I watch my teacher's face with care"

Yoshie Urakami, 12, is in her final year at her elementary school in Munakata city on the southern Japanese island of Kyūshū. Her favorite subjects are music and social studies.

There are 981 children at my school which is in Munakata, just outside the big city of Fukuoka. It is a brand-new school and was only opened four years ago. I suppose it is quite big for an elementary school – there is

Yoshie practises the piano after school.

one little school on the island of Okinawa which only has six pupils and one teacher!

I like my school very much. My class teacher is called Harada and she is very nice and kind. But best of all, we have a "Happy Friends' Wood" here. This wood was created by the combined efforts of teachers, parents and children in a small wood near the school. There are sports fields, an outdoor music theater, a viewing tower overlooking the surrounding city and lots of rare trees and flowers which we grow. Coming from a big city, I fell in love with the Happy Friends' Wood at first sight.

My favorite lessons are music and social studies; I am not so fond of physical education and sports. In class I watch my teacher's face with care and listen with attention. I don't talk much in playtime but once I start, I become very lively.

Let me tell you about our school year in Japan. The year begins with the nice spring weather in April. During this term lots of expeditions to the surrounding hills and parks are organized. We take packed lunches, and all the age groups go together. Our summer vacation is during July and August. It can get very hot and humid here in the summer. Many children who live in the big cities go to the beach or visit relatives in the mountains for their summer vacation.

We go back to school in September. The main event of this term is Sports Day. We have piggyback fights, races, relays and dancing. The competition is strong, and we are all very eager to score very well in the races. Autumn is the most comfortable season in Japan, so we all do our best to do our school work well. When the leaves are beginning to change color we know that winter is close at hand. Japan is a long country from north to south so there is a big difference in the severity of the winter. In the north lots of snow falls, but we hardly get any here.

The school closes again toward the end of December, and we all look forward to the celebrations of the New Year. We are given money and presents by our parents and relatives at this time. But it's soon back to school again for the winter term.

Luckily this is a very short term, and in the middle of March we get our spring vacation before being promoted in April.

My school day lasts from 8:30 in the morning to 4:20 in the afternoon. Some children in Japan are still kept very busy, even when they come back from school. There are many "After School Learning Classes" such as piano lessons, calligraphy practice and abacus classes. So it is a long and busy day, but we still find time to play. The boys play baseball and video games, and the girls play games such as tag.

At the moment I don't go to any "After School" classes. I go home and look after my younger sister until my parents get back from work. I occupy the time by practicing the piano and doing my homework. The rest of the evening is spent chatting with all the family together.

Do I have any ambitions? Well, I think I would like to be a kindergarten teacher best. I like small children, and I am quite good at looking after them.

Yoshie thinks hard before answering a question in class.

"My life is just making dolls now"

Shiun Fujimura, 70, has been making Japanese dolls for over fifty years. There are not many traditional doll makers left today, and Shiun's greatest wish is that his grandson should follow him into this highly skilled profession.

I did not particularly like dolls when I decided to become a doll maker. The year was 1925, and there was very little job choice for working people. There was no chance to go to high school then, so the work alternatives were restricted to laboring, taking a job in a store or becoming an apprentice to an artisan. I decided to work for a craftsman making dolls.

Doll making has long been a traditional skill in Japan. Male dolls are called *Ichimatsu* dolls, supposedly after a famous

After the different parts of the doll's body have been cast, Shiun applies three layers of skin-colored paint.

actor who lived several centuries ago. We still copy the likeness of his face on the dolls. We also make female dolls, and in the old days these used to be good companions for upper-class girls. All the dolls have real human hair and their kimonos are exact miniatures of real ones. Their designs have remained unchanged for centuries.

Like most apprenticeships, my training was long and hard. I was up at the crack of dawn cleaning floors and running errands, and didn't finish until 11:00 at night. There were even times when I got up to study my master's work while everyone else was asleep. Yet I think I must have had a knack for this trade because I never got totally fed up. One of the clearest things I remember from this time is receiving a whole collection of dolls from America. Out of courtesy we made gorgeous dolls for each U.S. state in return.

I trained for six years as an apprentice, and then had to serve two years in the army, so it wasn't until 1935 that I was able to set up my own business. My master had a good reputation as a craftsman, so he was able to get me enough orders during those first difficult years of going it alone. Things went well and I soon got married and eventually had five sons. Then came the upheaval of World War II and in all the chaos I thought doll making must be finished. But to my surprise a new market appeared when the fighting was over – American soldiers bought my dolls to take home as souvenirs!

Let me explain to you how we make our dolls. First of all, we carve separate wooden molds for all the different parts of the body. Then we make a mixture from starch and wood sawdust which has a texture and firmness like clay. This is pressed into the molds until it hardens, and then the castings are struck. The different parts of the body – the face, arms, legs and torso – are then colored with three layers of paint. We always try to get the finish to look like the slightly yellow Japanese skin color. It is often said that the life of a doll is in its eyes, and putting them in and painting them is the most highly skilled part of my work. The eyes are similar to the artificial eyes used for blind people, and even I, who have been doing this work all my life, get really tense when I am painting them. Finally, the face is drawn, and make-up and coloring for the cheeks applied and the hair fitted. Then the body, arms and legs are assembled. The finished, naked dolls are then dressed in gorgeous kimonos made by my daughter-in-law.

My life is just making dolls now. My wife died ten years ago and my eldest son also died some years back. I won't live much longer, and my greatest wish is to have a successor to carry on my work. Fortunately my grandson, Takashi, says he will become a doll maker. He is my hope and pleasure.

Three finished dolls. Can you see why getting the eyes right is so important?

"I may never see the clients I work with ever again"

Masako Yamamoto, 20, is a bus guide for a leading Tokyo sightseeing company. She lives in a company hostel in central Tokyo with other girls from her firm.

I have been working as a bus guide for two years now. The company I work for is called *Hato Bus* which is the leading sightseeing company in Tokyo. The tour buses are used both by visitors to the capital from the provinces, and by foreign tourists. As I am not fluent in a foreign language, I work as a guide for Japanese tourists.

I joined the company immediately after leaving high school. The job appealed to me because I wanted to do something to help people. Also, bus guides in Japan have to entertain their clients with songs between stops, and I love singing! So you see, the job suited me very well.

Eighty newly-graduated high school girls joined the company at the same time as me, and we all began a two-month training period. I had no experience of this kind of work before, so we all had quite a time trying to mimic the instructor. We had lessons in elocution, manners and the correct etiquette to use toward our customers. Then we were given guide books and told to memorize the simplest guided tour of Tokyo. The practices were actually done on a bus, and I found this really quite difficult, particularly as I was brought up just outside Tokyo and didn't know much about the famous places in the center.

When the training course came to an end I was given my first job. It was a four-hour tour called "Tokyo – a tour." I rehearsed it over and over again. The night before my first day I was so nervous I hardly slept. The next day was a holiday so the bus was packed, and my heart was thumping wildly as I began my talk. Once I got going, though, everything went well, and when I had finished all the customers clapped. That made me very happy.

Our company offers various excursions from a short four-hour tour to longer ones of up to eleven hours. Guides have to be on their feet for all this time, so it can get very tiring. When I first started I thought my calves were growing thicker, I was standing up so long! In spring and autumn we have a lot of schoolchildren on our tours. It

is customary in Japan for children to make a two- or three-day educational tour a couple of times during their school year. On these occasions, we usually spend some time out of Tokyo visiting Mt. Fuji and other sights in the surrounding area.

I live with the other bus guides in a company hostel in central Tokyo. The reason for this arrangement is so that our bus schedules can be as smooth and efficient as possible. When I finish a hard day's work it's fun relaxing with the other girls who share my room. We chat and sing, and exchange ideas about our work. On my day off I return to my parents' home in Hino City in the suburbs of Tokyo. There I can really relax and wash the strain of work away.

It's strange, really. I may never see the clients I work with again. But it gives me great pleasure to make my customers happy and contented. I'm always trying to improve my talks and think of new songs that they might like. I do this because I want to be a better bus guide and please my customers even more.

Masako poses for a photograph with one of her groups in front of the Nijubashi Bridge – the main entrance to the Imperial Palace.

Holding the tour company's flag on high, Masako leads a group around the sights of Tokyo.

11

"*Rakugo* is still alive in modern Japan"

Suzametei Bufa, 43, is a master storyteller – or *rakugo-ka* as he is called in Japan. He appears regularly on TV and in the Storytellers' Theater in Tokyo. He is married with two children.

I was born in the town of Noda which, as every Japanese person knows, is famous for producing soy sauce. My family has run a barber's shop there for many generations. My father was the eighth in a long line of barbers who passed on the business from father to son. My father wanted me to be a barber too, and was dead against my becoming a storyteller. So I bowed to his wishes and went to a hairdressing course and took a job in a barber's shop. However, I liked *rakugo* so much that I found it difficult to be enthusiastic about cutting people's hair. One day when I was working and lisening to *rakugo* on the radio at the same time, I became so absorbed by the story that I shaved off one of my customer's eyebrows by mistake!

I could see it was no use trying to be a barber, so I went home to try and persuade my father to let me take up *rakugo*. He refused to begin with, but eventually my mother managed to make him change his mind. So, at the age of 18, I came to Tokyo to train as a storyteller.

Rakugo are funny stories, many of which were composed more than a hundred years ago. They are performed by a single storyteller who plays the roles of many different characters. Part of the skill in storytelling is being able to mime different actions using only a few stage props – such as a folded fan or a towel. For example, a fan might be used to represent chopsticks or a sword. The *rakugo-ka* himself always wears a kimono and gives his performance formally, sitting at the center of the stage.

When I first came to Tokyo, I became a *zenza* – the lowest rank of *rakugo-ka* who are allowed to participate at performances. Our jobs were fairly menial – making tea for the senior pupils and masters, folding their kimonos and beating drums for the opening and ending of shows. We were allowed to do some storytelling, but only at the beginning of performances, before the main audience had arrived. It is difficult to act properly in front of a small audience, but everyone has to go through this disciplinary period to be a real *rakugo-ka*. In my day it was tougher than it is now as I had to live in with my master and do all his housework as well! Most pupils live independently today.

After three years as a *zenza* I was promoted to *futatsume* – the second lowest rank of *rakugo-ka*. I can hardly describe how happy I was at the promotion. It was a wonderful feeling to have somebody else to make tea for me and fold my kimono!

The art of telling funny stories is being able to mime many different characters, using only a few stage props.

Bright lights advertise the Storytellers' Theatre in Tokyo.

The highest rank a *rakugo-ka* can reach is called a *shin'uchi*. This is when he is allowed to take on pupils of his own. It is not until a storyteller reaches this stage that his work is truly recognized and respected by everyone. I reached this stage thirteen years after being made a *futatsume*.

Although society has changed a great deal since the art of storytelling was established more than a hundred years ago, *rakugo* is still alive in modern Japan.

"Even one accident prevented makes my job worthwhile"

Masao Izawa, 43, is a traffic patrol officer in central Tokyo. His job is called _Shiro Bai_ (white bike) in Japanese, and he sees his role as preventing accidents by making sure drivers obey all the traffic regulations.

I was 39 when I took my "white motor-cycle" license and started to patrol. "White bikers" are usually young, so I was quite a late starter, but there was a rather special circumstance which made me decide to join the patrol. This was my father's death in a road accident ten years ago. I have

Masao and his white bike on patrol in central Tokyo.

never been so furious in my life. How could my own father, a traffic police officer's father, die like that? Couldn't it have been prevented?

Ever since that tragedy, my horror and hatred of road accidents has mounted, so I decided to join the patrol. I thought that even if I could prevent just one accident it would make my job worthwhile. Unfortunately, the number of car accidents is increasing in Japan. There are more and more cars, motorbikes and trucks on the roads these days, but the biggest cause of accidents is that the drivers themselves do not obey the rules. The worst offenders are youngsters called _Bosozoku_. They are young motor-cycle riders who drive through the city at insane speeds making a terrific racket. They are a disgrace!

When we catch drivers ignoring speed limits or going through traffic lights, we immediately approach and warn them. It's the same in any society; a member must stick to the rules. If people start to ignore traffic regulations they are likely to

The busy roads and highways of central Tokyo have the highest accident rate in Japan.

go on and neglect other social rules as well. It's for this reason that we warn everyone, even if they are only guilty of very minor offenses.

I'm out patrolling on my bike for five hours every day – and sometimes more if road conditions are bad. My patrol area is central Tokyo, which has more accidents than anywhere else in Japan – about 30,000 a year. Around 70 percent of these are caused by speeding.

We are real professionals when it comes to speed. I can tell at a single glance if someone is exceeding the limit. We have special speed-sensitivity training where we learn to identify the color, make, speed and number of people in a car in a single instant. Of course, when we are actually booking somebody for a traffic offense we need proof, so we use speed recorders.

When we are trying to catch someone, we sometimes need to go very fast ourselves. As it would be unthinkable for a patrol officer to cause an accident, the examination and training to join the patrol is very strict. It takes a full year before a recruit is allowed on town patrol. He also has to be strong. A fully equipped white bike weighs around 300 kg (661 lb) and has rapid acceleration. I harden my body by practicing judo in my spare time – this enables me to handle a white bike at my age.

I would be much happier if our work was not needed on the roads, but that doesn't seem likely. So this afternoon I will be patrolling somewhere in Tokyo as a captain of a group of fifteen white bikes.

"It takes a year to learn to drink tea correctly"

Sado (tea ceremony) and *Kado* (flower arranging) have a very long artistic tradition in Japan. Fuku Kitayama has been teaching both these unique skills for many years.

I have always liked flowers, and I first began to practise *Kado* while I was still at school. I have been doing it ever since. *Kado* is the art of increasing the natural beauty of flowers by shaping and arranging them according to certain set rules.

Sado is the ceremony of drinking tea. It has more difficult rules of movement than *Kado*. In fact to learn how to eat the cake

Fuku demonstrates to her pupils the correct method of mixing the tea in the bowl.

served with the tea properly can take three months of practice, and it takes a year to learn to drink tea correctly. Moreover, to learn all the movements of the ceremony thoroughly – making the tea with a bamboo implement called a *chasen* and serving your guests correctly with tea and cake – takes at least several years.

Both *Sado* and *Kado* have a long history which stretches back at least six centuries. The reason why I took up both these arts is because both of them share the same principle – the respect for beauty. Art should not be separate from ordinary life – it is part of it. This is why I enjoy teaching these accomplishments to my pupils.

I worked as a secretary for six years before I became a teacher, and the manners and tact I learned in this job have served me well. Etiquette is very important in *Sado* and *Kado*, so I train my pupils very strictly. I see *Kado* as a hobby, really. It brings great pleasure to gaze at beautiful flowers, and to touch them with your hands. *Sado*, on the other hand, is really part of everyday life. It has its ordinary actions, such as putting on the kettle and cleaning up the tea room, but it also emphasizes the beauty of movement – this is why I spend so much time teaching the correct way to bow or to hold the tea bowl. And of course, my pupils have to practice over and over again before they can make tea correctly. It is not easy. But gradually, after much repetition, they begin to understand the right attitude needed for this ancient ceremony. Good tea utensils are also important for *Sado*. Indeed, some experts say that it is impossible to distinguish between a good and bad tea bowl until one has been practicing this ceremony for many, many years!

In the old days it was compulsory for all Japanese to become accomplished at *Kado* and *Sado*. Times may have changed, but people are still eager to learn. I teach fifteen pupils of all ages. We always finish with a pleasant chat after relaxing our minds with tea and flowers. Many things come and go in this chaotic world, but as long as we still treasure tranquillity of mind, *Sado* and *Kado* will live on among the Japanese.

Fuku looks on while her pupil arranges the flowers according to the rules of Kado.

"The ferries are a vital link between Japan's islands"

Mitsunaga Karimata, 48, is captain of the 4,500-ton ferry, *Sunshine Okinawa*, which carries passengers between Tokyo and Okinawa. While on duty he lives on the ferry, but his home is with his wife and children in Okinawa.

As you know, Japan is an island country. In addition to the four large islands – Hokkaidō, Honshū, Shikoku and Kyūshū – there are numerous smaller ones, and 440 of these are inhabited. Naturally, ships play an important role in such a country, and the ferries are a vital link between the islands, even today, in the age of the airplane.

I was born on the island of Okinawa, which is located right at the southern end of Japan's chain of islands. The island was occupied by the U.S. Army after World War II, and was only returned to Japan in 1972. I grew up surrounded by the sea, and had a vague feeling that I would like to spend my life working with it in some way. This idea was reinforced by my teacher at high school. This was about the time when Japanese trade was starting to expand, and he believed that the sea was going to be the most important means of development for Okinawa. So I decided to work for a shipping business there.

Mitsunaga's traditional wooden house on Okinawa.

The Sunshine Okinawa *sets sail from Tokyo on her long voyage south to the island of Okinawa.*

That was twenty-six years ago, and now I am a captain with my own ship, the *Sunshine Okinawa.* I sail on the 1,648-km (1,024-mile) run between Okinawa and Tokyo which takes us about fifty-two hours. My passengers are usually a mixture of vacationers visiting Okinawa for its sparkling sea and historic sites, and islanders traveling to the mainland on business.

As a captain, I live a very regular life. I am always up by 6:00 in the morning and the first thing I do is to check the weather. When the sea is calm I can relax, knowing that my passengers will have a comfortable voyage. Usually I am busiest when entering or leaving port, but when visibility is bad, or the sea starts to act up, my full attention is required on the bridge. I find I get twice as tired as usual at times like these.

One problem about spending so much of my life on board ship is that I have little opportunity to get much exercise. I have a lot of responsibility as captain so I cannot afford to be out of shape. I try to do regular morning exercises and go jogging whenever I am on shore. The ship's cook also makes sure I eat a good, balanced diet. I'm not fussy about food and will eat anything he puts in front of me! Such is the way I spend my days – a day in Tokyo, two at sea and a day in Okinawa.

The ferry company gives me sixty-seven days vacation a year. I always find it takes at least a week to get used to life on land after spending so much time at sea. While on vacation I enjoy playing golf and Go (a Japanese board game), but my greatest pleasure is relaxing with my family – then I can forget all about the routine of the ship.

It has not always been easy spending a life at sea. There was one occasion when a close relative of mine died, and I was unable to attend the funeral as I was in the middle of the Pacific at the time. But the sea is the career I have chosen for myself, and my aim is to finish my working life without an accident.

"People who love trains don't care about promotion"

Kazutaro Ohishi, 50, always wanted to be a train engineer ever since he was a child. He began his career driving steam trains, but has since become a regular engineer of the world famous "bullet train" — perhaps the most efficiently-operated train in the world.

The *shinkansen* or "bullet train," connecting Tokyo and Osaka, was opened on October 1st 1964. I had the honor to run the first train, nicknamed *Hikari 2*. I had been preparing for the day for a year beforehand, so I can truly say that I am one of the oldest *shinkansen* engineers.

As a child I always dreamt of becoming an engineer, and so I was delighted when the dream came true. I've worked for the Japanese National Railways for more than thirty years. During that time I have never been absent from work through illness. Even when I have a cold or do not feel well, I always begin to feel better as soon as I get into the engineer's cab.

When I began to work for the railroads after finishing high school, we still had steam locomotives in Japan. So the first kind of train I drove was a steam train. As you probably know, steam locomotives are driven by burning tons of coal. They need more than two tons to run 80 km (50 miles). The control of speed and power totally depends on how you burn the coal, so driving a steam train is quite a skilled job. In Japan, the number of steam locomotives started diminishing after 1965, and they

Kazutaro does his routine checks on his engine before setting out on a journey.

were completely replaced by electric trains in 1972. I gave up driving steam at an early stage in this transition, and ran electric trains for nine years. After that, I was put on the *shinkansen* trains and I have been running these for nineteen years.

There are more than a thousand engineers working on *shinkansen* lines. Two engineers operate a *shinkansen hikari* (the nickname for the faster service meaning "light"), and one engineer and one inspector are in charge of running a *shinkansen kodama* (meaning "echo"). Besides the engineer and inspectors, three conductors are usually on board, both for *hikari* and *kodama*. An engineer's working day is fixed at five and a half hours by JNR's working regulations. Roughly speaking, I shuttle between Tokyo and Osaka three times in six days and then have one or two days off. The engineers not only have to run the train from one terminal station to the next, but also to prepare the train for the journey at the depot.

At first *shinkansen* trains consisted of twelve coaches but now all the trains have fifteen coaches. More than 280 *shinkansen* trains run a day at peak time. They cover 170,000 km (105,636 miles) which is four and half times as long as the circumference of the earth. The distance that the trains have covered so far (up until April 1982) is 678,280,000 km (421,475,170 miles) – 1,764 times the distance between the earth and the moon!

All *shinkansen* trains are controlled by computer, so running a *shinkansen* is less interesting than driving a steam locomotive. However, the *shinkansen* can carry an incomparably larger number of passengers, so I feel a greater responsibility for seeing that they arrive at their destinations safely and punctually.

I have visited Europe a few times and have driven trains there. The French High Speed Train can reach 257 km/h (160 m.p.h.) and there are other trains that can reach 200 km/h (125 m.p.h.). However, I still believe that the Japanese *shinkansen* is the world's best railroad in terms of quality and performance. Also, there have been no fatal accidents in the whole nineteen years the service has been running. The *shinkansens* are very safe trains.

Most of my hobbies are related to trains. For example, I enjoy taking pictures and filming steam locomotives, collecting match-box trains and making miniature trains which can even carry passengers. Besides this, I enjoy piloting a small airplane. I got my license about ten years ago.

People like me, who really love trains, do not care about promotion. Engineers I met in foreign countries told me the same thing. I very much prefer an engineer's seat to going into management. I would like to continue to drive *shinkansen* trains as long as I can.

The famous bullet train thunders towards its destination.

"It is not robots that drive cars but human beings"

Nachisa Kubota joined the Nissan car company after falling in love with a sports car called Fairlady Z. He uses his skills to build safe cars, and is determined "not to be defeated by Mr Robot in the factory!"

Have you ever noticed Datsun cars in your town? Datsuns are made by a company called Nissan and are exported all over the world. I work for an associated company called Nissan Bodyworks Ltd. The factory is in the Kanagawa district, about 60 km (37 miles) outside Tokyo.

The Japanese car industry was one of the first to introduce robots and automation into their factories. I mainly work on a production line installing interior equipment in cars, such as instrument panels and so on. Part of the production line is controlled by robots; no human could rival their astonishing accuracy and speed. Well then, are humans needed at all? Of course they are! Final inspections and detailed work are still dependent on human judgement and long experience. This is especially true of car interior work, where human sensitivity to detail is crucial. After all, it is not robots that drive cars but human beings. The car is not much good unless the occupants are comfortable, and are able to drive it safely. If a person is empty inside, however handsome he is, he won't keep people interested in him. A car is the same. However marvellous it looks from the outside, if the interior is no good, it is not nice to be in it for a long time. Therefore, we install the equipment in each car with great care – as though it were our own.

One of the cars my company builds is a

Nachisa works on the interior of his favorite Datsun sports car.

sports car model called Fairlady Z. This is a wonderful car. She is known as a Datsun 280zx overseas. For a six-cylinder sports car it is cheap, and its road-holding capabilities are really excellent. Other remarkable things about this model are its streamlined body shape and its sun-roof. At any rate, I joined this company because of my fascination with this car.

When I was a high school student, I was not certain when and where I would look for a job. I am the youngest in my family and my elder brothers were all employed locally, so I thought of going somewhere else instead. Meanwhile, a job representative from Nissan Bodyworks came to our school with a brochure of Fairlady Z, then the new model. When I saw the car, I thought to myself — that's it! A company making such wonderful cars must be a good one! The more I thought about it, the more my desire to get a job in the company increased. I had a driving license but knew nothing about cars. Fortunately I passed the company entrance examination.

Since then I have been closely involved with this fascinating car every day. Such a long relationship makes me regard her as a lover. Fair enough, her name is Fairlady. The car is sold all over the world, so production goes on day and night. I work on two alternate shifts. One week I work from 8:00 a.m. to 5:00 p.m. and the next I work from 8:00 p.m. to 6:00 a.m. It was a little difficult to get used to this at first, but now my body's rhythm has become accustomed to the routine.

I pay great attention to my body — a factory worker's body is his capital. Compared with the old days, manual work is not as heavy and vigorous as it used to be. Still, if you are not physically fit, work cannot be done, so I relax on non-working days and I eat good balanced meals. Occasionally I engage in sports and tune up my body.

I am not sure how long we will continue to make Fairlady Z, but even when I have to start on a new model, I hope to carry on making safe and comfortable cars. I think this is the hope and wish of all Nissan workers.

Sports cars waiting at the docks to be shipped to Europe.

"It's up to me to manage the land of our ancestors"

Masae Sugesawa manages a small rice farm in the mountainous Nagano district of Japan. Her husband works for a local company and her son lives in Tokyo, so she works the farm by herself.

The district of Nagano where I live lies in the center of Honshū – the main island of Japan. My farm is surrounded by high mountain peaks, and the winters can be very severe, with temperatures dropping well below freezing. Fortunately, my village rarely has a heavy fall of snow, but if there is a freak storm it makes it very hard to get down to the town to buy food. The climate in summer is cool and fresh, and our occasional visitors from Tokyo are always thrilled by the clear mountain air.

So, it is up here in the mountains that I manage my 60 hectares (150 acres) of rice paddies. To be precise I should say *our* rice paddies, but as it happens my father is very old, my husband works at a dam construction site nearby and my son and his wife have moved to Tokyo. So, with the way things are, it's up to me to manage the land of our ancestors as best I can.

Despite mechanization, which has made farm work easier, many people no longer want to work on the land. Young people, especially, reject farm work and

The mountainous district of Nagano where Masae's family have worked their rice farm for generations.

leave for the cities. Husbands, too, may earn more in the towns, and this often leaves the housewives like me to do most of the farmwork. This tendency has become a big problem in the farming world.

I'm up by 5:30 at the latest every morning. My husband has to leave for work at 7:00 a.m., so I cook breakfast and do all my cleaning and washing before leaving home for the rice paddies by 8:00 a.m. My rice plants are marsh plants so they always need to be covered with sufficient water. The first thing I do every morning is to check the water level, as the water I let into the fields the previous day often disappears overnight. When this happens I open the sluice gates and get the level back to normal as soon as possible.

The busiest times of the year for rice farmers are at planting time in early summer, at the weeding season in mid-summer, and at harvest time in the autumn. During these periods I usually work in the fields right through the day until dark — perhaps stopping once for a chat with neighboring wives over a cup of tea.

In my village, planting time takes place around mid-May. Once we start we cannot stop until it is all done, whatever the weather, or we will miss the right time. After this we work full speed on the weeding through June and July. We spray weed-killer, but the weeds seem to emerge as fast as we spray. Still, if we left the weeds and neglected to spray our plants against disease, all our previous hard work would turn into water bubbles! When the plants are ripe we cut off the water supply to the paddies and the harvest begins. With the help of a combine harvester, which is shared by all the farms in the village, we usually finish the harvest in ten days. And that is the end of rice farming for the year.

When the cold winter wind blows over the land I am free from outside work. Then even I have time to enjoy my hobbies. I knit toys and clothes for my family and it is a great privilege to enjoy a cup of tea sitting round the warm stove with my friends.

I have been living this life ever since I was married. It is certainly true that farming is not an easy life and I cannot blame young people for preferring the bright lights of the city. But I love this land, and wish to continue farming as long as my health permits.

Weeding the paddy fields can be back-breaking work.

"Judo develops the mind and body together"

Yasuhiro Yamashita first started judo when he was 9. Since then he has been champion of Japan several times and champion of the world twice. He combines judo with research work at Tokai University in Tokyo.

I was born in the Kumamoto district of Kyūshū – the southernmost of Japan's main islands. In traditional Japanese folklore, people from this part of the country have been called *mokkasu*, which means stubborn or hard to please. I'm afraid this is right in my case. From an

early age I was unyielding, stubborn and extremely rough. I was big even as a child at kindergarten – as big as children in the second and third grade of primary school. Unfortunately my size and muscular power caused some problems in the playground. Sometimes fights would get out of hand, and, without intending it, I would hurt others and make them cry. So when I was 9, my mother decided to send me to the local judo school where I could let off steam.

Judo, like karate and kendo, is one of the Japanese martial arts. The big difference between these activities and modern sports is that in the martial arts, the spiritual side is very important. In judo we improve our skills by repeatedly practicing attacking or defending movements, and the aim is not only to increase our physical strength, but our spiritual strength as well. This is the way that the martial arts have been used to train body

Many hours of practice are necessary to master the different holds.

Both physical and spiritual strength are needed to succeed at judo.

and soul for centuries. They are still very popular today.

For someone like me who loved to be active, judo was most suitable. I started to practice enthusiastically and after only four months I won the Kumamoto Judo Tournament. From then on I never looked back. In a few years I became the best in Japan for my age and people started calling me "Monster Child." At about this time I moved to the Kanagawa district near Tokyo in search of the best school to develop my judo. I also enrolled in Tokai University to continue my studies. In my second year here I won the All Japan Judo Tournament. Then in my fourth year all my dreams came true and I won the World Championship title. Since then I have held the All Japan title for six consecutive years, and the World title twice.

It's now fifteen years since I first started judo. It's difficult to continue anything so long, and especially difficult when it is something as demanding as judo. Although practice is important, it is not good enough just to put in a lot of hours. What counts is the amount of mental and physical concentration you put into your practice in a set period of time. It is not possible to win with muscle power alone. To bring one's strength into play one must have physical and spiritual power. This is the fascination and charm of judo and is the reason why I have devoted all my youth to it.

My day begins at 6:30 a.m. and I am already hard at work by 7 o'clock. I take a break mid-morning to do my research work at the university and continue my judo practice at 4:30 p.m. for a further three hours. Altogether I suppose I average about five or six hours' practice a day.

I wish to continue judo all my life. And my ultimate ambition? To win a gold medal at the next Olympic Games.

"I never take extended vacations"

Hiroshi Asagi worked very hard for six years as an apprentice cook before buying his own restaurant in central Tokyo. He specializes in *tempura* – a fish and vegetable dish which is very popular in Japan.

Have you ever tried *tempura*? *Tempura* is one of the most popular dishes in Japan. It is made from different kinds of seafood and vegetables which are coated in a flour mixture and then fried. It sounds easy, doesn't it? But in my opinion to coat the fish and vegetables in the flour mixture requires as much attention and skill as is needed to make a lady's dress. Otherwise, why was it necessary to undergo an apprenticeship for six long years?

When I was still at high school, my father's tire business went bankrupt, and although I was able to continue my studies for a while, it soon became obvious that I would have to get a job to help out with the family income. One day I ate a dish of *tempura* in a restaurant. It was delicious! The next thing I knew I had got a job as an apprentice at a local restaurant. It had a very good reputation for *tempura*, but the training was old-fashioned and hard.

I worked from 8 o'clock in the morning until midnight without a break. For the first two years I wasn't even allowed to touch *tempura*. Instead I was given all the dirty jobs – cleaning the garbage cans and lavatories and grating vegetables. Later, I was allowed to arrange the food on the

Hiroshi and his mother pose proudly outside their little restaurant in Tokyo.

dishes, cut up pickles, cook rice, make egg-soybean curd and make up the raw fish dishes. Finally, after three years, I was allowed to fry *tempura*.

It was a hard apprenticeship. There was no fire even in winter and the kitchen floor under our work area was frozen. Yet I put up with it. I wanted to have my own restaurant, so I was very eager to learn.

I became independent when I was 24. I had no money to buy my own restaurant so I had to bow my head to the bank and ask them for a loan. With this I was finally able to open a restaurant called "Tenasa." It is so small that it is full with sixteen customers.

When I first opened I owed so much money that I worked non-stop. I didn't close the restaurant once in a month. Even now I never take extended vacations. Nor do I employ anybody, but manage the hard physical work with help from my father and mother. It has been like this for twelve years, but there have been no bad moments.

My day starts at 7:30 a.m. when I go down to the local fish market to buy prawns, eels, squid and various kinds of fish I need for my recipes. I return to the restaurant around 10 a.m. and prepare for the lunchtime opening. We are open from 11 a.m. to 3 p.m. We then have our own lunch and prepare for the evening session from 5 p.m. to 9:30 p.m. When business is good we can expect around sixty customers a day, but when it is bad this can fall to around forty. I like my customers. My restaurant is in central Tokyo which is where ordinary people live. Whole families often come to eat with me, and everyone is interesting and friendly.

I usually take a day off on Thursdays. My favorite recreation is to go for a long swim and then relax afterwards with a cup of *sake* (rice wine). Swimming brought me a wife too. I agreed to teach a young lady who sometimes came to my restaurant to swim, and we got friendly. I found out that she worked as a designer. Now the difference between a designer and a *tempura* cook is like the difference between water and oil, so our friends said that ours was an "international marriage!"

My dream is to own a restaurant in one of the really smart parts of Tokyo. Please come and have a meal at my restaurant one day!

Many different kinds of seafood and vegetables make up a good tempura *dish.*

"All over the world religious beliefs are in danger"

Tsusho Nukino, 32, is a Buddhist priest who administers his temple in Tokyo and preaches the teachings of Buddha. He also advises people who run away from home or who have domestic problems.

I am a priest of the Buddhist Temple, and am called *Obōsan* by people in Japan. Buddhism is one of the great religions of the world. It was founded in India in the fifth century B.C., and gradually spread out across Southeast Asia, through China until it eventually reached Japan. As it spread it was influenced and changed by the different countries it passed through. Today there are Buddhists in Europe and America as well.

Let me explain in plain language the difference between Buddhism and Christianity. Christ is an absolute being, but the Buddha, who is the equivalent of Christ, is not thought of as divine. He is more of a teacher who taught how people should live harmoniously together, and in this way become closer to God. Humans are weak. They grumble and complain about hardships, and often make grave errors when their eyes are blinded by money and power. My job is to teach the ways of Buddha to these confused people.

I was born a priest's son and went to a Buddhist university to learn about my religion. After graduation, a student who wishes to become a priest must go through special training before he is allowed to administer a temple. To begin with, he must receive the Buddhist commandments from his master; in my case, my father. Then he must go through a hard period of self-denial, getting up at 4 a.m. every day to learn the duties of being a priest.

The severest training takes place in deepest winter. The young priests shut themselves in the temple for a hundred days, and through a vigorous program of physical self-denial, deepen their understanding of Buddha's ways. Rising at 3 a.m. and not retiring until midnight, they pour cold water on themselves every three hours, seven times a day, to purify their body, and then sit formally reading the *sutras*. Food is served twice a day, but it is only soft, watery rice. The idea of these trials is to conquer the desires of the body, such as hunger, sleeplessness and pain.

I had to endure all this training before attaining my present position as one of the priests administering this temple in Tokyo.

My daily routine begins with the morning service in the temple. The majority of the Japanese people believe in Buddhism, but there is also another religion called Shinto in Japan. This is an ancient community religion with local shrines for household and ancestral gods. Buddhism and Shinto are not a threat to each other — they exist together. For example, most weddings are conducted in Shinto shrines, whereas funeral services are usually Buddhist ceremonies. I may conduct several services for the dead during the day. I also have a pastoral role to play — giving advice to runaways and those with domestic problems. I have even been made a godfather to an abandoned baby! The day ends with the evening service and the solemn chanting of the *sutras*.

One of the great problems today is that all over the world religious beliefs are in danger, and Japan is no exception. Yet I believe the spiritual support religion can provide is more important in the modern world than ever before.

The quiet gardens surrounding this Buddhist temple are an island of tranquillity amidst the bustle of Tokyo.

Tsusho at prayer in his temple.

"English is so difficult, only a few master it"

Tsuneko Tashiro teaches English at her local middle school. She and her husband, who is also a teacher, live in the old mining town of Fukuoka. They have two sons.

Fukuoka was a flourishing mining town until twenty years ago. Then it straddled the largest of all the southern coalfields. But now oil has taken the place of coal as our main energy source, and the mines are closed and the town has become quiet.

One of the results of this change is that there are now fewer children in school than when I first started teaching. In the Japanese educational system children go to elementary school from the age of 6 to 12, middle school from 12 to 15, and high school from 16 to 18. The first two levels are compulsory for all children. I am an English teacher in the local middle school. I teach 21 hours of classes a week – 15 hours of English and the rest morality, club activities and "leisure time."

There were two main reasons for my decision to study English. One was that I wished to travel abroad. I am rather shy

about admitting the second reason. At my high school we had a very handsome English teacher whom I adored. I think this might have had something to do with

Much of a teacher's time is spent in preparing lessons and marking written work.

my enthusiasm for English!

I usually get to my school by 8:00 a.m., ready for the first leason at 8:15. I'm afraid the Japanese are not very good at learning foreign languages. English, particularly, is so difficult that very few master it. It is so different from Japanese in pronunciation, grammar and so on. So my English lessons are often quite a struggle, both for me as the teacher and for my pupils.

I also take classes for "leisure time," when we work together in the school garden. We teach the children to grow various kinds of vegetables and learn the joy of a close contact with the earth. They do not often get this opportunity to work with nature in their ordinary lives.

School finishes at 4:45 p.m. but there are all sorts of odd jobs that keep me busy until about 6:00. Then I hurry home to cook supper for my husband, who is an elementary school teacher, and my two sons. Life can be very hectic with so many commitments! The evening meal is very important to us, despite the rush I some-times have to get it ready. It is the one time of day when the family is all together and we can chat about what we've been doing. For the rest of the evening I do my marking and preparations for the next day's classes. The busiest period is towards the end of term when I have reports to write and exams to mark. Then the work piles up like mountains!

Generally, people think teachers are privileged to have long summer vacations, but for half this time we have work to do at the school. Even if we do go away, we have to write to the headmaster for permission to do so. During term-time my day off is the time when I change from being a teacher to being a housewife. During the

Tsuneko attempts to explain to her class the baffling nature of English grammar.

day I deal with all the household chores and relax in the evening by reading a novel, or answering letters to my old pupils. My most enjoyable moment happens once a fortnight, when my husband and I go shopping in a neighboring town. At last we really have a chance to talk to each other!

"Use every moment of every day without wasting it" is my motto.

"In Japan everyone has a camera"

Hajime Yamamoto sells one of Japan's most famous industrial products – the camera. He works in the export department of Asahi Optics Trade Company in Tokyo, but has spent some time abroad on assignments for his company.

Have you ever heard of a camera called Pentax? The first single-lens reflex model was developed in our country in 1952. Ever since then, Pentax cameras have become more and more sophisticated, as more advanced electronic technology is applied to their production. Today, the camera is known all over the world, and it is my company that makes and sells it.

I work in the export department. My main job is to decide how many of each type of model we should export to our offices overseas. I am head of the business section of my department, so I have a lot of

Pentax's modern factory outside Tokyo.

Pentax cameras being assembled on the factory floor.

responsibility to see that the day-to-day running of the office goes smoothly.

My day starts at 8:00 a.m. when I arrive at my office. The first thing I do is to go through the telexes that have come in from branch offices both at home and abroad. These are usually concerned with requests for stock, so I check with our factories to see if they can supply the requested amount. Another important part of my job is to study how our competitors in the camera industry are doing, and how our prices compare with theirs. Very careful planning is needed to make sure that we get our production and marketing programs right. Big meetings, when all the directors and the heads of overseas offices attend, are held twice a year, and this is when we do all our long-term planning.

In Japan everyone has a camera – and I mean *everyone*, not just one camera per family. I think one of the reasons for the camera's popularity is that today so many good models are fully automatic. This means that you no longer have to be an expert photographer to take good pictures. All camera makers are now competing to develop light, easy-to-use, low-priced cameras, and the big retailers are also cashing-in on the camera fever by enlarging their storefronts and display areas.

I have always been interested in cameras, though I can't say that the mechanical aspects are really my strong point. As a child my special hobby was taking photos of pretty flowers and developing the prints. Today, my favorite pastime is relaxing in the park with my children. My special dream is to return to West Germany one day. I was assigned there for seven years with the company and the magnificent natural scenery of the countryside made a deep impression on me. I keep the sweet memories of that time in the lens of my heart forever!

"The Japanese are very concerned about their health"

Kimiko Haraguchi, 32, is a young mother of three girls and a "full-time" housewife. She lives in the Tokyo suburb of Saitama with her husband, her parents and her grandmother.

I am a housewife living in Saitama, which is a northern suburb of Tokyo. The Saitama area is quite flat and used to be an agricultural area producing mainly rice, but today it has been transformed into suburbs. When land prices in Tokyo soared, more and more people bought cheaper land in Saitama and commuted into Tokyo. This is the reason why Saitama was suburbanized.

My family have been farmers for generations and our house is still surrounded by some rice fields and farmland – though there are now many more houses than before. My husband is 32 years old and we have three daughters – the eldest one is 7. We live with my parents and grand-

Four generations of Kimiko's family sit down to a feast together.

mother. These days the size of Japanese families has become smaller and smaller, the average size being about four. My family, which consists of eight from four gererations, is big by Japanese standards.

My husband works in a bank. I worked in the same bank when I left high school. After a few years I met my husband, who was very active and lively. As I have one younger sister but no brothers, my parents adopted him as their heir when we got married.

My house is an old two-story building which was built more than a hundred years ago. It has three traditional Japanese rooms, two Western-style rooms and one kitchen. By Japanese standards the house is big, but as there is not much storage space, we would like to have it rebuilt in the future. In Japan, most families have their own house. The quality of houses has been drastically improved recently, and they can no longer be described as "rabbit hutches" as they were in the past. Nevertheless, they are still not as big on average as European or American houses.

I usually get up at six o'clock and prepare breakfast. Washing, cleaning and shopping are my main chores, which I do after my family leaves for work. In the afternoon I take my daughters to piano, calligraphy or swimming lessons by car. I start preparing dinner at about half-past six. Each generation likes different sorts of food, so it is difficult for me to satisfy the whole family. For example, my daughters like hamburgers, curry, and corn soup; my husband likes *tempura* (fried fish and vegetables) and meat; and my parents like traditional Japanese stew. After dinner, I wash the dishes and send the children to bed around nine o'clock. After they go to

bed I can finally relax watching TV and chatting with my husband and parents. It is not until about half-past eleven that I go to sleep.

One of the things Japanese people are very concerned about is their health. That is partly because the cost of our health care has sharply increased, but a more significant reason may be that the quality of everyday food has got worse, and that they lack physical exercise. I did not bother doing physical exercise, because I thought I was too busy with the housework. However, I realized I needed more exercise so I joined a volleyball club organized by housewives in my town.

Apart from health, what worries me most is our family's living expenses. Although my husband's salary rises regularly, our family's financial situation is deteriorating, because inflation is higher than pay raises. Therefore, housewives like me have to be thrifty. Despite these financial difficulties my nature is rather optimistic, so I am not too worried. I like to enjoy life.

Our desire in the future is to get our house rebuilt and to give our three daughters a university education.

Shopping for bargains at the supermarket.

"My motto is 'always be modest'"

Shigeru Kobayashi, 36, works as a journalist on the *Hokkaidō Times* – a local paper which serves the people of the most northerly island of Japan. Although he finds his work very demanding, Shigeru enjoys the rapport he shares with his readers.

My father was a plumber and my mother was a primary school teacher. Just after I was born my family moved to Hokkaidō, which is the most northern island of Japan. The climate in Hokkaidō is very harsh and cold in winter, but the countryside is wild and beautiful, unlike other parts of Japan which have been developed and urbanized.

Since my parents were both working, I was brought up by my grandparents. I do not know why it was so, but I was a fairly spoiled and naughty boy. After finishing high school, I studied journalism at a university in Tokyo. Then, I came back to Hokkaidō to become a news reporter for the *Hokkaidō Times*. To begin with, I worked in the editorial office and my special assignment was to write stories and reports about the police. It was through that job that I met my wife who was working in a police station at the time.

I first wanted to be a journalist when I was a child, partly because the reporters I came across in TV dramas seemed to have a very attractive life-style. However, when I became a journalist I found that there was an enormous gap between idealized TV reporters and actual ones. A lot of jour-

Shigeru gets his story ready to go to press.

nalism consists of chasing around after news stories and this can be quite physically demanding.

Three years later I was given the job of covering the Sapporo Winter Olympic Games. These first years were not always a success, and I have to admit that on occasions I seriously thought about changing my job. However, when I started getting letters from my readers which showed that my articles were being appreciated, I became more enthusiastic and minded less about the demanding hours.

Japan has been described as a nation of readers. There are 126 daily newspapers in the country, and the total daily circulation is about 44 million copies. This

Sports events, like this local powerboat race, are the sorts of stories a good local reporter must follow up.

means that every household reads, on average, 1.27 newspapers a day. Like Britain, Japan has "national newspapers" with circulations extending all over the country. These account for about half the daily circulation.

As my newspaper is a local one, it does not have many opportunities to publish sensational articles. What we try and do is to cover news that is closely related to the needs of our local community. My guiding principle is "always be modest," and this is what I try to be in my contribution to the paper and to the local people.

"A luxurious kimono costs more than 1 million yen"

Kimiko Okuda, 76, runs a kimono shop in Sendai on the southern island of Kyūshū. Kimonos are traditional Japanese costumes and are still in great demand for ceremonial and festive occasions. Kimiko is helped in the shop by her four sons.

All the shops that deal in kimonos are now called *gofuku-ya* shops. Many years ago there were also *futomono-ya* shops which sold only inexpensive kimonos made from cotton or wool. In those days, before the last war, *gofuku-ya* was the name used only for the shops that dealt in formal clothes made from silk. But once Western clothes became popular, *futomono-ya* disappeared and *gofuku-ya* started to sell cotton and woolen kimonos as well.

My late husband's family ran a *gofuku-ya* shop for more than a hundred years in Kyoto. I married into the family fifty-four years ago at the age of 22. Kyoto is one of the most traditional towns in Japan with numerous temples, shrines and historical remains. Kyoto is also the center for kimonos. One street in particular – Muromachi Street – is famous in the kimono trade. Merchants from all over Japan buy their kimono cloth from here.

My husband and I left Kyoto with our four sons and opened the present shop in Sendai just after the end of the last war in

1945. My sons all work in my shop. These days the main department stores and big clothes shops also sell kimonos. In the old days it was more usual for people to buy kimono cloth from merchants who called at their home. The kimono merchants had to know their customers' tastes and bring rolls of cloth which were likely to suit them. There are still quite a few shops selling kimono cloth this way and my shop is one of them.

My shop employs about thirty salesmen and they start visiting their customers around ten o'clock in the morning. Each has his own customers, and must be absolutely familiar with their tastes, so that they trust him. Usually, a customer will ask us to bring several rolls of cloth and then will choose one or two patterns from them. My shop also employs six full-time tailors and forty-four part-time ones, who sometimes work for other shops as well. In a nutshell, then, what my shop does is to sell cloth, arrange for a tailor to make up the kimono and then see that the finished

Kimonos are still worn on many festive occasions in Japan.

article is delivered.

What most surprises foreign tourists visiting my shop is the high price of kimonos. A kimono for a girl celebrating her *seijin-shik* – the traditional ceremony to mark her coming of age – normally costs as much as 500,000 yen ($2,150) and some luxurious ones cost more that one million yen ($4,300).

Although there are few opportunities to wear kimonos these days, Japanese women still like to have them – though most do not get given dozens when they get married as happened in the old days.

I believe kimonos are not only practical clothes but also an "art," because of their traditional gracefulness and beauty. We should be proud of them.

A customer is fitted with a beautiful kimono. Kimonos of this quality can be very expensive.

"It's tough climbing up and down mountains all day"

Shigehito Katagir, 31, comes from a family of foresters in the mountain village of Tatsuyama. Shigehito studied forestry at a university and then returned to his village to work for the local forestry cooperative association.

My village is called Tatsuyama, and lies in the mountains above the River Tenryu. It is only a small village with a population of around 2,300, and its main industries are forestry and tea growing. My ancestors have been growing trees around the village for the past 500 years. The main species we plant are cedars and cypresses. In each

Shigehito at work felling trees in the forest.

hectare (2.5 acres) we plant 2,500 to 3,000 saplings in a neat checker-board pattern. It takes between 40 and 60 years for these to grow big enough to be used as timber, so we are really planting them for our grand-children's generation.

My family have always been foresters. After studying forestry at the university, I returned to Tatsuyama to work for the village forestry cooperative association, while my father continued to look after our family forests. Forestry cooperative associations have been set up all over Japan where forestry is practiced. It is easier for a group like this to organize the purchase of saplings, the maintenance of paths through the forest and the selling of timber, than it would be for an individual on his own. Our village cooperative has certainly contributed to the industry and prosperity of the area.

I began by working in the office, dealing with the business side of forestry. Then, two years ago, I was asked to be in charge of the section concerned with the cutting and planting of trees. Ever since, I've been up at 6:30 a.m. every day (except when it rains) to dash off to the part of the forest where we are working.

The places where we usually work are high up in the mountains – often 500 to 800 meters (1,640 to 2,625 ft) above the village. As they are not accessible by car, we have to walk part of the way – it can be tough climbing up and down mountains all day! Young trees need careful tending if they are to produce good timber later. Much of my work is spent clearing away the grass and plants growing around them and trimming off the branches to lessen the number of knots in the wood.

I used to get exhausted when I first started this job. Sometimes I would be so tired that I went straight to bed after finishing dinner. One soon gets used to it though.

I suppose you would say I lead a very quiet life compared with the bustle of the city. There are no discos or bars in the village, but it has the advantage of being free from jostling crowds and complicated human relations which characterize a place like Tokyo. I am quite content because I enjoy the outdoor life. My hobbies are hunting and fishing, and I always carry my rods in my car so that I can fish anytime on the way back from the forests.

However, this life doesn't suit everyone. Sad to say, the population of my village had declined steadily since the 1950s, as more and more people have migrated to the cities. But I think my job is very important. Although Japan has a beautiful natural environment, its preservation is now endangered by the rapid development of heavy industry. The trees and plants provide water and oxygen which are indispensable for all creatures on the earth. Planting and growing trees is also of great importance in terms of preventing rivers from flooding. So, even if all the other people in the village left, I would still stay to look after the forests.

Tea and traditional Japanese stew make a welcome midday break for the forestry gang.

"Drawing the letters is as important as the finished work"

Sohshin Morinaga, 51, teaches calligraphy to classes of both children and adults. He also edits a monthly magazine on calligraphy and produces his own avant-garde works.

Calligraphy is one of the most important cultural traditions in Japan. It is an art form centered on painting letters, and its origins go back many thousands of years. I first became interested in it while I was still at school, but at that time I never thought it might one day be my career.

Sohshin sets to work on some of his own avant-garde calligraphy.

However, as time went by I became more and more interested in this art form, and today I find myself teaching it to about fifty adults and children a week! Besides my teaching, I also edit a monthly magazine on calligraphy for artists and enthusiasts. It has a circulation of about 2,000 copies and is financed by the readers. Then of course, I have my own work to do.

There are several different schools of calligraphy in Japan. I belong to an avant-garde group called *Keisei Kai*. This does not mean that I have abandoned classical calligraphy altogether. My work is a variation on the old skills, and is still based on classical forms and styles.

Perhaps the most difficult thing to grasp about calligraphy is that the actual drawing of the letters is as important as the finished work. In other words, the action of forming the letters with the hand, and the shape of the brush strokes, is an art form in itself. Calligraphers express everything in the few seconds or minutes it

Many children in Japan attend calligraphy classes after their main school lessons are over.

takes for them to complete their brush strokes. This is what makes calligraphy so different from painting. Painters can spend any length of time they like working on a picture. They can paint a bit, reflect on what they've done so far, stare out the window, make corrections or even repaint. Once calligraphers start drawing, they must continue to draw in one long flowing movement until they have finished, without a pause. This is why calligraphy can be both psychologically and physically exhausting – particularly if one

is drawing really big letters.

I try to explain all this to my students, but it is difficult for them to understand all the concepts at once. I have discovered that too much high-minded talk on the "artistic" nature of the act of drawing can put off people just starting to learn calligraphy. This is why I concentrate on the practical side of drawing at first.

"Being a model is not all glamor"

Eri Shiraki is a model who works for television commercials and magazines. She is 19 and lives in Tokyo, but gets the chance to travel widely in Japan through her work.

About five years ago, when I had just started my first year at high school, I was spotted by a man from a modeling agency while I was shopping in town. This lucky break was the beginning of my career in modeling.

My first job was to pose as a cover girl for a girls' magazine. In Japan there are forty-three different girls' magazines on the market. All of them have sections on fashion and show business, and include the usual love stories and interviews with celebrities. It was the first time I had posed in front of a camera and I can still remember how nervous I was. I tried hard to give the impression to the readers that I was their friend, as the magazine was aimed at girls of my own age.

There are two types of work for models in Japan. One is fashion modeling, which is mainly done for shows and fashion magazines. Models who are tall and slim are best suited for this. The other is commercial modeling for brochures, TV commercials, magazines and posters. I am a commercial model.

I do most of my work for television. Apart from our national station – the Japan Broadcasting Corporation – there are five major commercial television stations and many smaller ones. So, whenever you turn on TV, you can be sure of a choice of seven or eight different channels. The majority of these programs show commercials, so you see, there is quite a demand for models.

I start to prepare for a job the day before the actual filming. I make sure the clothes I will be wearing fit all right and check when and where I am expected. I always try to sleep well to prepare for work. The following day I arrive at the film set, meet the staff and wait for my turn to go before the cameras. There are always professional people to help me dress and do my make-up. It is a very satisfying moment when the filming goes off without a hitch and the staff all thank one another for their efforts.

But being a model is not all glamor, in

Eri has a quick snack at lunch time.

fact sometimes it can be quite hard. On occasion I have to pose outside in thin summer dresses in the middle of winter, or conversely, wear thick winter garments under a blazing sun. Perhaps the most disappointing experience is when a commercial you have worked hard on together, and seems to have gone well, is found unsatisfactory by the sponsors. The film is then put on the shelf forever.

But mostly I have happy memories of my work. The nature of my assignments gives me the opportunity to visit various exotic places in Japan which other people might not have a chance to see. I also get the chance to meet famous people.

Of course, the working life of a model is not all that long, so I want to make the most of it. I never forget my good fortune in getting the job — in Japan good jobs for women are still hard to come by. But above all, I never wish to forget the wonder of the smile which I learned through my work.

Eri models the latest casual wear, set against a nautical backdrop.

"Nuclear weapons must never be used again"

Michitada Takasugi belongs to the Japanese Socialist Party. He is a member of the Upper House of the Japanese Parliament – the National Diet – and has strong views on disarmament.

The National Diet consists of two houses, the House of Representatives (the Lower House) and the House of Councillors (the Upper House). The Lower House has 511 members and the Upper House has 252 members – all elected by popular vote. I am a member of the House of Councillors and I belong to the Japan Socialist Party, which is the present opposition.

I was just 20 when Japan was defeated in World War II. I saw my country in ruins and in a state of confusion. Being a sensitive and idealistic youth, my sense of responsibility was strongly awakened. I thought that the work of rebuilding this defeated country was up to the young to carry out. Japan started the war and was defeated. We saw the pictures of the hell at Nagasaki and Hiroshima after the atom bombs were dropped. We shall never repeat this mistake again. We must build a peaceful society so that we will never see nuclear weapons used. This is why I decided to go into politics as a socialist.

When I graduated from college I took a job as a secretary to a member of the House of Councillors. This was my first step forward in the world of politics. I was elected a member of the House in 1974, and have been a member ever since.

A politician's life is a very busy one. I get

Michitada contributes to a major debate on disarmament in the House of Councillors.

up at 7:30 a.m. and immediately go through the newspapers and the news on TV. Every other day I have a breakfast meeting with other members and we exchange our ideas. There follow official meetings and committee work until the House convenes at 10:30 a.m. When the work of the House is finished I go back to the official residence for members of the House and have dinner. But even after dinner there are policy research meetings and so on waiting for me, and it is not unusual for work to continue until midnight.

As a member of the House my present job is chairman of the special Price Countermeasure Committee. The job of this committee is to examine ways of stabilizing prices and combating inflation. So we tackle all sorts of price problems from food to gasoline. Fortunately, in the last two or three years, Japanese prices have been very stable compared with those of the U.S.A. and Europe. I feel happy and proud that this is partly as a result of our hard work. I am also involved in encouraging social welfare works for the aged, the disabled and children.

On Saturdays and Sundays the Diet is closed so I return to my home in the Ibaraki district. But I do not go back home to take a rest. I go back in order to listen to the opinions of the people who elected me and I talk to them. I cover every corner of my area on my own feet. I believe it is a basic political duty to talk to people and to reflect their views in national policy.

At first glance, all this work may seem like a drop in the ocean when compared with the huge problems facing the world today. But it is only by long and consistent effort that good results are reached in politics. As a politician I feel the weight of responsibility heavier than ever before.

The Diet building containing the two Houses of Parliament.

"Japanese industry has a tendency to think 'shrink'"

Mikio Takahashi, 37, works as a design engineer for Sony in Tokyo. His job involves designing cassette players, such as "Walkman", and improving their quality.

Have you ever noticed people walking about with headphones on, listening to music in the street? The device they use is called a "Walkman," a small tape recorder. I work for Sony Sound Ltd, the makers of these, in their main office in Tokyo. My job is to work on designs for the Walkman's components. More than half a million of these miniature tape recorders have been sold already, though I never expected it to sell so well. At the trial manufacture stage, the opinion of the majority of people in our company was negative about the thing. Despite all that, our company chairman decided to put them on the market.

The chairman's judgement proved to be wonderfully right. Now the Walkman is exported to 170 countries and is popular worldwide. But the Walkman is not the only product made by Sony. Our main products are video machines, tape recorders, TVs and stereo systems.

Sony has grown to be a huge company, but when it started it was very small. It began in 1946, with a work force of only twenty people. There was no laboratory, and the employees worked hard making tape recorders.

I joined in 1968, when Sony was smaller than it is today. Now, fourteen years later, we sell five time more than when I started.

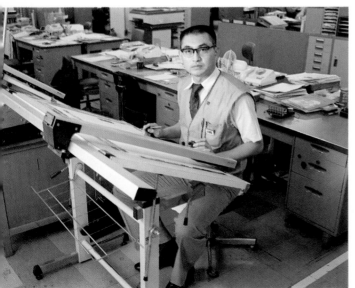

Mikio at his desk in the design department of Sony Sound Ltd.

Sony has factories in the U.S.A., England, West Germany and many other countries. Its employees number over 20,000 and there are many associated companies.

What is the reason for Sony's huge success in only thirty-seven years since the war? There are probably many reasons, but Sony's policy never to imitate others has certainly contributed to its achievements.

Japanese industry has a tendency to think "shrink." That is, to make things smaller, thinner, lighter and cheaper. This was the principle applied to tape recorders which were Sony's first big success. This was followed by radios, color TVs, cassette tape recorders and the Walkman. Indeed Sony's history can be summarized as a process of miniaturizing large machines without loss of quality.

I generally get to the company by 8:15 a.m. to start work at 8:30 a.m., and usually finish at 6:00 p.m. My work is concerned with improving the marketability of products already produced by the design department. Our task is to think of ways to commercialize them. When work time is over, I often work overtime, so I don't usually get back home until nearly 7:00 p.m. Then my family of four settle down to eat supper cooked by my wife.

My wife and I live with my two parents. Our house is built of wood and is very old by Japanese standards. Usually wooden houses only last for twenty years or so. My house was built 150 years ago when wood was used for the foundations. The wood is very sound, and with a little repair here and there can even stand up to earthquakes.

I can trace my ancestors back about 300 years. They were farmers, and the result of this is that we own a large piece of land in what is now the heart of Tokyo. My father

A small selection of the tape recorders and stereo systems that have made Sony famous throughout the world.

grows trees and shrubs and acts as a wholesaler for gardeners. I help him with the digging on my vacations.

By the way, what do you think my hobby is? Well, it is also to play with tape recorders – old open-reeled types. My greatest joy is to record classical music from radio broadcasts on tape, and then to edit them. In my room I have many machines just like in a music studio, and I have 1,300 classical music pieces on 800 reels of tape. The music that I have chosen to record has to reach a certain standard so that I can listen to it many times.

My hopes for the future are to have children soon, and to try to work on video tapes.

"Not many company managers work with ordinary fishermen"

Toshio Tamaka, 58, runs a fishing company which operates in Sagami Bay, 60 km (37 miles) south of Tokyo. He still manages to help on the boats every day, despite having a busy office to run.

Japan is made up of many islands, so it is not surprising that fishing has always been an important industry. Indeed, the Japanese have a reputation for enjoying sea food more than any other food – half the total amount of animal protein eaten in Japan comes from fish. Sagami Bay, where I run my fishing company, contains a rich variety of different fish species. Because of its geographical closeness to Tokyo, the bay plays an important role in supplying the metropolis with food from the sea.

I started my fishing company thirty-six years ago. I needed a large amount of money to buy big fishing nets and motorized boats, so I went into partnership with some friends of mine. I'm sorry to say that we didn't do very well to begin with, as none of us had much experience in fishing. The debts began to pile up and eventually my partners abandoned the enterprise and left me to carry on alone. It took a lot of hard work to make the company profitable, but I succeeded. The company has had its ups and downs, of course, particularly at times when the price of fish fluctuates wildly. At times like that, catching too many fish can be as unprofitable as catching only a few, because a big haul brings the price right down. Things are going reasonably well at the moment, though, and I can afford to employ fifteen people.

Fishing boats on the quayside at Sagami Bay.

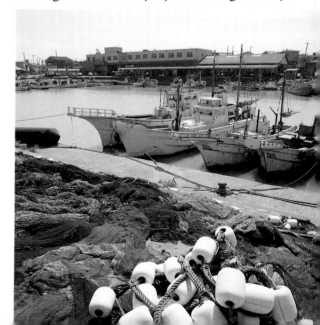

Sorting the catch for the morning market.

There are three main types of fishing in Japan. The first type is coastal fishing where the boats go out and return from the fishing grounds on a daily basis. This is the type of fishing we are engaged in. Much bigger operations are carried out by the deep-sea fishing fleets. Boats sail as far as the Arctic and Antarctic Oceans to hunt whales and to trawl. Another important area is off the African coast. This section of the fishing industry has been badly affected by the fishing restrictions in territorial waters that many countries have imposed since 1977. Indeed, the number of fish caught in this way has halved in the last ten years. The final sector can be described as off-shore fishing. This is generally operated by medium-sized boats run by relatively big companies.

I get up every morning at 3:30 a.m., which is usually before dawn. We leave the harbor at 4:00 a.m. and arrive at our fishing grounds about half an hour later. The fishing method we use is called *teichi ami*. It consists of stretching nets a few kilometers offshore in a box-shaped pattern to catch the shoals of fish that swim into them. Hauling in the nets takes about an hour, after which we return to the harbor to sort the catch for canning or taking to the market.

Auctions at the fish market begin around 7:00 a.m., and then I can go thankfully home to have my breakfast. The rest of my day is spent attending to the business side of my company and dealing with the affairs of the local fishing association, of which I am chairman.

It is a tiring day. Generally I just flop in front of the television in the evenings, before going to bed around 9:00 p.m. On average I don't sleep more than about six hours, which isn't much is it? But I go to sleep very easily and sleep very deeply, so I do not feel tired in the morning. Not many company managers would get up at the crack of dawn to work with ordinary fishermen, but it is my principle to work hard. Besides, I enjoy it.

"I try very hard to become the characters I act"

Manjiro Ichimura, 33, is a much acclaimed *Kabuki* actor. *Kabuki* is one of Japan's most popular performing arts, where old stories are acted out on stage using specially stylized dialogue and actions.

Kabuki has a history of more that 300 years. It has a number of special characteristics which distinguish it from other stage performances. The actors are always dressed in the most gorgeous kimonos, and traditional white make-up is worn. Perhaps its most unique feature is the absence of actresses – male actors play all the female parts. When they do this it is called *Onnagata*.

An actor who has a slim physique, like a woman, is most likely to play *Onnagata*. If he is well built, on the other hand, he acts male roles called *Tateyaku*. If, like myself, an actor is in between, he plays both *Onnagata* and *Tateyaku*. But until the body is fully developed, every actor plays *Onnagata* at least once, in order to learn amorous sexuality and sweet tenderness.

In the *Kabuki* world, family connections are much respected. If a father is a *Kabuki* actor, his son may well follow him on to the stage. My father is a *Kabuki* actor, and I am his second son. My first appearance on the stage was when I was 5 years old. For those of us who were born and raised in *Kabuki*, it is no problem to fit in, but it is very difficult to become a part of this world if a person has only decided to become a *Kabuki* actor after graduating from college.

As a child, I could act quite innocently, but as I grew older certain thoughts began troubling me. I liked science at school and I wished to go on with it. In the end I became an actor through my brother's misfortune. My elder brother, who was a *Kabuki* actor, became seriously ill and was told by doctors that he would never be able to go back to the stage again. Fortunately, he recovered and is still active as an actor, but at the time, I thought if I did not go on the stage there would be no son to follow in the family tradition. I don't regret this decision. I would never have become a good actor if I hadn't enjoyed performing.

I started to learn to dance at the age of 6, and was also taught *Naguata* (singing) and *Samisen* (a three-stringed musical instrument). I was trained very strictly, and I

think my acting is sharper and more lively as a result of it.

A *Kabuki* actor's life is very varied. We do different performances every month, so our routine of rehearsals and plays changes accordingly. Our season runs for ten months and then we take a vacation.

I do my own make-up, which is very white and unique in *Kabuki* style. It only takes about fifteen minutes as I am used to

Manjiro on stage during a climactic scene in a Kabuki drama.

doing it. The paints and the way the eyebrows are drawn make my face very different, so I look into the mirror intently to see how I can put more personality into the part I am playing.

It is already twenty-eight years since I first appeared on stage, but I have never once regretted being a *Kabuki* actor. I have played many roles, and my motto is to try very hard to become the characters I act.

The special make-up used in Kabuki plays an important part in the uniqueness of the drama.

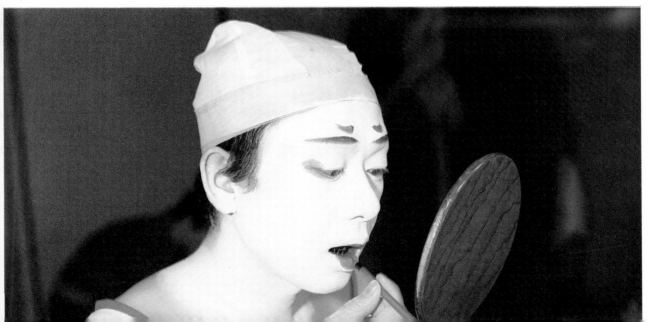

"I always try to develop my pupils' creativity"

Hisayo Yanegawi, 26, is an elementary school teacher in the seaside town of Hiratsuki, just south of Tokyo. After three years' experience, Hisayo finds she is beginning to come to grips with her teaching, and is starting to enjoy it.

I have been a teacher for three years now. There are about 25,000 elementary schools in Japan coping with about 11 million pupils, though this number is falling as the birth rate declines. I believe a similar trend is taking place in most Western European countries.

My first year as a teacher zipped by like a dream, but I think I'm now beginning to get my ideas on teaching worked out. Elementary school education comes at the most important time in a child's development. This is why I think it is so important to develop my pupils' creativity — particularly as this is a characteristic that some people think the Japanese lack.

Before I became a teacher I wanted to be a painter. After high school, I took an art teaching course at college. It was while I was learning how to teach children to paint that I decided to make teaching my career rather than painting. To begin with, I had only intended to teach art, but I soon got interested in other subjects as well — that's why I became an elementary school teacher, so I could teach all subjects. I think it's only by teaching everything that I can develop children's creativity in every field.

Most of an average day is spent either in

For one child at least, school is quite a joke!

56

teaching or its preparation. I get up at 5 o'clock in the morning and take my dog for a walk. I then get down to preparing my lessons for the day. My first class is at 8:30 a.m. My class is made up of second-year pupils, and I teach Japanese, math, history, geology, science, music, art, physical education, ethics and *yutori*.

Let me explain to you about *yutori*. Our education system puts great emphasis on vigorous intellectual training. Consequently, every school has a number of children who cannot keep up. To solve this problem *yutori* hours were introduced to offset the intellectual work with something a bit more relaxing. So in these hours teacher and pupils get involved in recreational things, such as various kinds of sports and games, caring for animals, growing plants and playing music.

After the fourth lesson of the morning, lunch is provided at the school for all the pupils and teachers. The children bring their own napkins from home and spread white tablecloths over their desks in the classroom to make lunch tables for groups of six children. I eat with a different group each day. This is my opportunity to really get to know my pupils, and to listen to what they say about themselves, their friends and their lessons.

You might think that once my lessons are over for the day, my time is my own. I do try to leave a few hours free in the evening, but I often find that I get bogged down in school work. This means that I do not have enough time for my own painting, and this makes me rather depressed.

But teaching *is* an interesting job, though at the same time a tantalizing one. I feel that the more you know about it, and the more experience you have, the more there is still to learn. I have my own problems with discipline and getting my lessons right, but then, there is no profession without its difficulties. I must be more positive, because once I have overcome these problems, I think I shall be a good teacher.

At lunchtime, the children quickly convert their classroom into a cafeteria.

Facts

Capital city: Tokyo.

Language: Japanese.

Currency: Yen; 233 yen = about U.S. 1$ (as of February 1984).

Religion: No single religion is recognized by the State. Buddhism is the main religion with a following of 80 percent of the population, with Christians comprising slightly less than 1 percent. Shinto is a Japanese community religion which compliments Buddhism.

Population: 118,390,000 (1982 census). About 76 percent of the population live in cities, and 58 percent of these live in the "Big Four" metropolitan areas – Tokyo, Osaka, Nagoya and Kitakyushu. Japan's population density is 300 persons per square kilometer – one of the highest in the world.

Climate: The climate is temperate with plentiful rainfall, as Japan is at the northeastern end of the monsoon area. Summer is warm and humid and winter is mild and sunny, except in northern Japan which can have heavy falls of snow. Spring and autumn are the best seasons with balmy days and bright sunshine.

Government: Japan has a hereditary Emperor, but since the Consitition of 1946, sovereign power has rested with the people. Legislative power lies with the Diet (Parliament) which has two houses elected for four years by direct, universal, adult suffrage. The two houses are the House of Representatives with 511 members and the House of Councillors with 252 members. For the purpose of local government, Japan is divided into prefectures (47), cities, towns and villages, each with their respective assemblies.

Education: The education system is divided into five stages: kindergarten (age 3–6), elementary school (age 6–12), middle (12–15), high (15–18), and universities whose degree courses are normally 4 years. Education is free and compulsory between the ages of 6–15. In addition to the State schools, private schools are found at all stages of the system, and are particularly important in catering to infant education and advanced education. At all levels of the educational system, scientific and technical education is an important part of the school curriculum.

Housing: Strenuous efforts have been made since 1945 to relieve the serious housing shortage that then existed and to improve standards. Today a sufficient number of dwellings exist and the problem has shifted from a question of quantity to one of quality. Over-population in the cities means that housing space is restricted, and the cost of accommodation, both private and rented, is very high.

Agriculture: Owing to the mountainous nature of Japan, only about one-sixth of its area is available for farming. The main crops are tobacco, tea, potatoes, rice, wheat and other cereals – rice is the staple food of the people. Japan also has extensive orchards for fruit growing, and forestry, including the famous lacquer wood of Japan, is also important.

Industry: Japan is the most highly industrialized nation in the Far East, with the whole range of modern light and heavy industries, including cars, electronics, metals, machinery, chemicals, textiles, cement, pottery, glass, rubber, lumber, paper, oil refining and shipbuilding. Almost 90 percent of the total labor force is engaged in non-agricultural industries.

The Media: Radio and television are as highly developed in Japan as anywhere else in the world. The NHK, or Japanese Broadcasting Corporation, operates 788 radio stations and 5,788 television stations (1979 figures). There are also 17 commercial radio companies, 57 television companies and 36 combined radio and television companies. Progress in TV technology is expanding rapidly, with stereophonic sound and bilingual broadcasting already available. The Japanese are also great readers. There are 126 daily newspapers and every household reads, on average, 1.27 newspapers a day.

Glossary

apprentice A young person who learns a trade or craft under the direction of a skilled worker.

avant-garde Artists, writers and musicians whose work is experimental or in advance of accepted methods.

calligraphy Artistic handwriting produced with a brush.

casting An object that has been shaped by being pressed into a mold.

disarmament The reduction or abolition of war weapons by a country or group of countries.

etiquette The correct code of behavior observed by a particular society or profession.

exports The goods sent out of a country for trade purposes.

inflation A situation in which prices are continuously rising.

kimono A loose robe with wide sleeves and a broad sash, worn as traditional costume in Japan.

martial arts Literally means warlike sports — judo, karate and kendo are examples of Japanese martial arts.

production line A factory system where goods are assembled on a continuous conveyor belt system.

shift A period of work. Used when an entire day is split into work periods.

Shinto Ancient community religion of Japan.

sponsor Someone who promises to support another person or group in an activity. In the television world this means someone who puts up the money to make a TV program in return for advertising time.

stage props Any article which an actor may use during his performance on stage.

sutra Buddhist holy text or prayer.

telex An international telegraph system usually used for communicating between businesses.

Acknowledgements

The publishers extend their thanks to Mrs Alison Chapman at the Language Centre of the University of Sussex, and to Mrs Etsuko Mosely and Mr Nori Morita for the translation of the manuscript.

PRONUNCIATION

Many Japanese sounds are like English.

Vowels

A is pronounced as "ah" in "father," but short and crisp.

E is like "a" in "day."

I is as in "hit," but a little higher in pitch.

O is like "owe," but without the final "we."

U is like "u" in "put," but spoken without rounding the lips.

In Japanese there are no diphthongs and in a succession of two or more vowels, each vowel is pronounced clearly and distinctly with equal length.

Consonants

B is like b in "bag," but spoken less explosively.

Ch is like "chi" in "China."

D is like "d" in "dog," but with the tip of the tongue touching the back of the upper teeth.

F is spoken as "f" in "foot," but sticking out your lips.

G is like "ng" in "singer."

H is like "h" in "hit" or "hue."

J is like "j" in "judge."

K is as "k" in "key."

M is spoken as in an English "m."

N is pronounced in two ways: first, before a, e, o, and u, N is spoken with the tip of the tongue touching the back of the upper teeth; secondly, N before "i" is pronounced as in the English "news" with the tip of the tongue touching the back of the lower teeth.

P is like the English "p," but less explosive.

R is spoken with the tip of the tongue touching the back of the upper teeth. It is similar to the English "l."

S is as "s" in "song."

SH is like "sh" in "ship."

T is like the English "t," but pronounced with the top of the tongue touching the back of the upper teeth.

W resembles the English "w," but is spoken without protruding the lips.

Y is the same as the English "y."

Z is pronounced like "ds" in "beds" or "z" in "zero."

Index